Nyam Thyme

A MODERN COLLECTION OF JAMAICAN RECIPES, HACKS, AND CULTURAL INSIGHTS

Nyam Thyme

A MODERN COLLECTION OF JAMAICAN RECIPES, HACKS, AND CULTURAL INSIGHTS

CHEF JACQUI FRANCIS

ARPress

ILLUMINATING IDEAS,
EMPOWERING VOICES

ARPress
45 Dan Road Suite 5
Canton MA 02021

Hotline: 1(888) 821-0229
Fax: 1(508) 545-7580

Ordering Information:
Quantity sales. Special discounts are available on quantity purchases by corporations, associations, and others. For details, contact the publisher at the address above.

Printed in the United States of America.

| ISBN-13: | Softcover | 979-8-89389-119-5 |
| | eBook | 979-8-89389-118-8 |

Library of Congress Control Number: 2024909323

To my husband, children,
and the land of my birth.
This is for you!

Dedication

This book is dedicated to my children, Wendi-Ann and David, who inspired me to write this book. They say parents are supposed to teach their children, but I learn so much from you both each day.

Acknowledgment

My deepest gratitude to my husband, Lance. I appreciate you so much. Your interviews during the writing process served me well and ensured that I got it right. You are the "wind beneath my wings."

I am extremely grateful to Janet McIntyre for your invaluable contribution, suggestions and insights, who always provided me with encouragement and patience during this project.

Maurine Capleton, my best friend and sister who always has my back. I am deeply indebted to you for your untiring support and belief in my abilities. Your constructive criticism, insightful suggestions during this project is second to none. I love and cherish your unwavering friendship.

Judith Zaidie, your unparalleled support, ingenious suggestions and extensive knowledge on food and wine pairings is truly appreciated. You will always be my wine connoisseur advisor.

My deepest gratitude to Wayne Paisley for providing all the pictures from Jamaica, and for your deep knowledge on the progressive food culture of Jamaica.

Vaughan Grey, I am grateful for you and your finishing touch. Your deep knowledge of the progressive food culture of Jamaica served to deepen my cultural insights.

I would like to also acknowledge and thank the following persons:

David DeYoung and Krystyna Garcia of Office Max Store, The Woodlands
Christine Marcus – Johnson
CherryAnn Donigan
Dureen Forrester

A Note from Jacqui

Feeding people is my love language!

For close to 40 years, I have shown how much I love my family, friends, guests, and patrons with my meals. There's a little piece of my heart in every plate that leaves my kitchen. Food cooked with love and from the heart can nourish the body and bring warmth and comfort to the mind and soul.

In Jamaica, where I am from, "nyam" means "to eat" and thyme is an essential ingredient in making jerk. So, I've put these two words together to create a Jamaican play on the phrase "time to eat." I hope that *Nyam Thyme* allows you to make time-saving, delicious meals so that all the variations and translations of the phrase "time to eat" brings excitement and joy to whomever you feed. I can see it now, people rushing to grab a plate of the meal you have prepared from one of the recipes I've shared with you. I dedicate *Nyam Thyme* to my husband Lance and my children Wendi-Ann and David, for whom I have enjoyed cooking throughout the years.

As a mother, entrepreneur, and immigrant, I believe in the rights of all people to live with dignity in an equitable world. Therefore, I am honored to donate 10% of my net profits from the first three years of sales of Nyam Thyme to the Tahirih Justice Center. The Tahirih Justice Center is a national non-profit organization that provides legal services, policy, advocacy, and education to serve courageous immigrant survivors of gender-based violence. You can learn more about them at www.tahiri.org.

I will also use proceeds to support an early childhood center in Lilliput, Jamaica. Lilliput is a small village in St. James, and education is the only way out for the children.

Walk good,

Jacqui

Jacqui's love for food began with her mother and grandmother who were great cooks and loved to entertain with their tasty dishes.

Her passion grew even more when she went to work at Grace Kennedy in 1978, the largest food company in Jamaica, where she was mentored by James Moss-Solomon, Company Director, who taught her the value of fine quality foods.

In 1986 her love affair with catering began because of her love for entertaining and pleasing her guests. She created the concept of a mobile hotel service that brought the finest standards of Jamaican cuisine to the table in private homes.

In 1995 Jacqui was invited to Jamaica House (Jamaica's White House) to be the Executive Chef for the Prime Minister of Jamaica. For 10 years her cuisine has graced the tables of state dinners for heads of states from all over the world. She has had the pleasure of cooking for Queen Elizabeth Il and her husband The Duke of Edinburgh, Princess Anne as well as CARICOM leaders

She was nominated "Best Caterer" five years in a row by the Jamaican Observer, the national newspaper of Jamaica. Jacqui's recipes have been published in several newspapers and international magazines.

In 2007 Jacqui moved to Houston, Texas. She craved the familiar tastes of her island nation. She felt compelled to share her passion and love for food. In 2010 she opened a restaurant, aptly named "Jamaica House" in Houston. Her goal was to expose the finer side of Jamaican culture and cuisine, so custom dishes were created using her signature sauces and seasonings allowing customers to have an authentic experience with Jamaican cooking using the freshest ingredients to create tasteful blends reminiscent of the flavors that reflect Jamaica's diverse heritage. The Jamaican heritage includes a mixture of Asian, East Indian, and African cultures. The customers' reaction to the sauces and seasonings was phenomenal.

JAMAICAN CULINARY TRADITIONS

If I were to write about all the things Jamaica is famous for, this would be an anthology. However, Jamaican cuisine is why you're here. For decades, the pots that have bubbled in the kitchens of plantations, our grandmothers, restaurants, and cookshops (take-out eateries) have enticed all who have come in contact with the aromas, Pavlovian as they waft through the air.

Throughout the culinary world, Jamaican cuisine is enigmatic. We have a rich oral history, so many of our recipes are passed down that way. Many of us learned our skills at the knees of a grandparent or parent. But just as the people are warm and inviting, so is our food. A plate of jerk chicken with buttery rice and peas is like a hug from a best friend you've longed to see. A hot beef patty is an enthusiastic hello, beckoning you to join in on the tasty fun.

Jamaicans are a proud bunch! Whether we are on an Olympic track, making music, or in the kitchen, we want the world to see our passion and embrace our rich cultural heritage. After all, Jamaicans have been charged to advance "the welfare of the whole human race," and its food is one of the easiest ways to do that.

Jerk is a style of cooking native to Jamaica, in which meat is dry-rubbed or wet marinated with a hot spice mixture called Jamaican jerk spice. It was developed by the Maroons—a group of Africans who escaped enslavement and inhabited the densely forested mountains of Jamaica. They live independently and maintain their rich African heritage through food, dance, music, religion, and language.

The Maroons use whatever natural food sources—herbs, spices, wild animals—that were available to them. They created the spicy dry rub, which, together with slow cooking over embers, help to preserve the meat allowing it to be easily transported as they move throughout the mountains, further evading enslavers.

Today, locals and tourists like to visit the Boston Jerk Center near Port Antonio, Portland. Fun fact: the parish is known for its lush greenery and deep turquoise waters.

To visit an authentic local Maroon settlement and discover the real origins of Jamaican Jerk, one must pay a visit to Moore Town, located at the very top of the hills north of Port Antonio. A trip to Jamaica isn't complete without embracing the island's rich history.

Table of Contents

Salads, Soup and Stews 3

    Island Style Caesar Salad...5

    Cool Calypso Salad...7

    Jacqui's Homestyle Chicken Soup.....................................9

    Jamaican Style Red Peas Soup – Easy Peasy Version! 11

    Jacqui's Roasted Carrots..12

    Cultural Insight: Soup Nights..13

    Jamaican Creole Shrimp Gumbo......................................15

    Buss-Yu-Belly Stew Peas...17

    Cultural Insight: Stew Peas Wednesday.............................19

    Jacqui's Succulent Oxtails..20

    Orange Sauce..22

    Cultural Insight..23

    Curry Goat..25

    Quick Black Ben and Corn Salad.....................................26

    Cultural Insight: No Goat, No Party................................27

Crowd Pleasers...29

    Jacqui's Saucy Twist for Any Meal...................................31

    Ackee & Cod Fish 33

    Jacqui's Quick Quiche...34

    Cultural Insight..35

    Tropical Charcuterie Board..37

Meat, Fowl and Seafood 39

    "Way To A Man's Heart ..." Pork Chops..........................41

    Jerk Shrimp & Lobster Jamdown.....................................43

    Mouthwatering Jerk Ribeye Steak.....................................45

    Jacqui's Lovable Lamb Chops...47

    Jacqui's Jammin' Jerk Chicken..49

    Jamaican Jerk Marinade..50

    Cultural Insight..51

Jacqui's Fall-Off-The Bone Jerk Ribs...53

Jacqui's Hack: Quick Reggae Ribs 54

Jacqui's Hack: Quick Jerk Chicken 55

Jammin' Salmon...57

Jacqui's Piquant Jerk Wings..59

We Jammin' Jerk Burger 61

Breaded Lamb Chops 63

Jerk Chicken Tortilla 65

Moreish Side Dishes..67

Festival Rice...69

Jacqui's Jamdown Rice & Peas...71

Cultural Insight: Traditional Jamaican Sunday Dinner 73

Jacqui's Ultimate Mac & Cheese...75

Zesty Orange Cornbread 77

Drunk Plantain 79

Variations of Cheesecake...81

Basic Cheesecake Recipe 83

Mango..85

Mango Glaze..85

Pineapple Cheesecake..86

Pineapple Gaze..86

Guava...87

Guava Glaze...87

Desserts..89

Sweet Life Bread Custard 91

Brie Cheese in Puff Pastry 92

Cultural Insight: Bread Puddin' 93

Rum Sauce 95

Tropical Ambrosia 97

Thirst Quenches 99

    Sorrel Sangria 101

    Mango and Guava Tropical Delight 103

    Carrot Juice 105

    Rum Punch 107

Wine Pairings for Jacqui's Recipes 109

Jammin' Jerk Sauce 111

Sweet Reggae Sauce 113

Cultural Insight: JaMex Cuisine 115

Cultural Insight: Port Royal 116

A Visit To Jamaica 117

Peppa Thyme..119

The Origins of Jerk 120

Culinary Insight..121

Best Food Spots To Visit 2024 122

S Hotel: A Jamaican Oasis 123

References for Jacqui Francis 127

Reviews..129

"If You Can't Take The Heat, Take The Sweet"

"I have had the unparalleled pleasure of enjoying the tasty concoctions from Mrs. Francis and therefore am able to vouch that these sauces and seasonings are truly authentic Jamaican products. Savor the flavors from J.G. and enhance your palate with the robust taste of Jamaica."

P.J. Patterson

Former Prime Minister of Jamaica

Salads, Soups and Stews

Island Style Caesar Salad

Island Style Caesar Salad

Ingredients

2 cups chopped lettuce

2 tablespoons Caesar dressing

2 teaspoons parmesan cheese

½ cup croutons

1 tablespoon J.G. Jammin' Jerk Seasoning

Directions

1. Place chopped lettuce in salad bowl.
2. In a separate bowl whisk together, Caesar dressing and J.G. Jammin' Jerk Seasoning.
3. Drizzle mixture over lettuce and sprinkle parmesan cheese on top.
4. Place in refrigerator for 3-5 minutes before serving.
5. Top with croutons.

Cool Calypso Salad

Cool Calypso Salad

Ingredients

1 large cucumber, chopped into bite-size chunks
1 bag spring mix or chopped lettuce
1 large mango, slivered
1 each red, yellow and orange bell peppers, slivered
1 small pack of cherry tomatoes
1 bunch of fresh basil
1 cup fresh or canned pineapple, cut in bite-size chunks
1 red onion diced
½ cup grapes, cut in halves
¼ cup cranberries
¼ cup walnuts
¼ cup bleu cheese or your favorite cheese crumbles

Vinaigrette dressing

2 cups orange juice
½ cup of sugar
½ cup lime juice
1 cup olive oil
½ teaspoon of salt
2 teaspoons J.G. Jammin' Jerk Seasoning

Directions

1. In a medium bowl, whisk together all ingredients.
2. In a large salad bowl, add vegetables with half of the vinaigrette dressing and mix gently to combine.
3. Refrigerate for no more than 3-5 minutes before serving.
4. Pour balance of vinaigrette in a small bowl for extra servings.

Jacqui's Homestyle Chicken Soup

Pro Tip: Don't forget!

Having a bowl of soup will fill you up before your main meal.

Leftover soup makes an easy, quick and nourishing lunch the next day by adding chicken broth and more vegetables.

Jacqui's Homestyle Chicken Soup

Ingredients

6 boneless, skinless chicken thighs, cubed

½ of a small kabashi squash, peeled

1 tablespoon fresh ginger, grated

6 cloves of garlic, minced

3 tablespoons green onions, chopped

1 tablespoon fresh grated turmeric or 1 teaspoon ground turmeric

2 teaspoons fresh thyme, chopped

3 teaspoons J.G. Sweet Reggae Seasoning

1 habanero pepper, (optional)

2 cubes chicken bouillon

½ teaspoon salt

2 large carrots chopped

4 small corn on the cob

Directions

1. Place chicken thighs in bowl and season with J.G. Sweet Reggae Seasoning, salt, and chicken bouillon.
2. Place peeled kabashi squash and chicken thighs in a large stock pot with 1 cup of water. Bring to a boil over medium heat for 10 minutes.
3. Remove kabashi squash and blend with garlic, pepper and 1 cup of water.
4. Return to pot, and add 2 more cups of water. Bring to a boil.
5. Add corn, ginger, turmeric and thyme. Stir and simmer 15-20 mins.
6. Add more seasoning to taste if necessary.
7. Garnish with chopped celery.

Jamaican Style Red Peas Soup – Easy Peasy Version

Pro Tip: Don't forget!

Label and date containers (use freezer - safe containers)

Ladle cool soup into containers leaving ½ - 1 inch head space on top.

Soups can be stored up to 3 - 4 days in refrigerator and 2 - 3 months in the freezer.

Any longer you risk losing freshness.

Jamaican Style Red Peas Soup – Easy Peasy Version

Ingredients

2 cans red beans or black beans

½ teaspoon of your favorite hot sauce (optional)

1 can coconut milk

1 envelope of Goya Ham Flavored Concentrate

2 sprigs fresh thyme

2 teaspoons fresh garlic, minced

1 cube chicken bouillon

1 teaspoon J.G. Sweet Reggae Seasoning

2 cups water

1 cup cooked andouille sausage (optional)

Directions

1. Combine all ingredients in pot and bring to a boil.
2. Simmer on medium-low for 10-15 mins.

Jacqui's Roasted Carrots

Ingredients

    20 unpeeled carrots, cut diagonally
    3 tablespoons extra virgin olive oil
    kosher salt
    freshly ground pepper
    3 tablespoons chopped fresh dill

Directions

1. Preheat oven to 400°F.
2. Toss olive oil with the carrots.
3. Sprinkle liberally with salt and pepper and place on a jelly roll pan.
4. Cook for 20 minutes.
5. Remove from oven and garnish with fresh dill and serve.

Cultural Insight: Soup Nights

Jamaicans are known to have certain meals on designated days of the week—and Saturday is the day for soup.

One would think that living on such a hot island, hot soup wouldn't be welcomed. But Jamaicans utilize a host of ground provisions such as dasheen, coco, yellow yam and cho-cho, to name a few, along with meats such as pigtail, chicken or beef bones to make the most tasty and hearty soups anyone could imagine. Yes, whatever meats (along with its bones) are left over from the week's dinners are used to make soup on Saturday.

Red Peas Soup is by far one of the most desired but it takes a long time to prepare, often times requiring a pressure cooker to get the pig tails just right.

Jacqui provides you with a quicker and easier hack to a Jamaican favorite!

Pro Tip: Don't forget!

This is a great recipe to make ahead of time.

Allow to sit in the refrigerator 1 to 2 days before eating. Substitute shrimp with 1½ cups of cubed chicken.

Jamaican Creole Shrimp Gumbo

Jamaican Creole Shrimp Gumbo

Ingredients

2 tablespoons olive oil

½ medium onion

2 large carrots, chopped

2 bell peppers, cored and chopped

4 cloves of garlic, minced

1 sprig thyme

1 can (15 ounce) diced tomatoes

4 cups chicken broth

1 pound uncooked shrimp, peeled and deveined

2 links chicken andouille sausage

2 cups fresh parsley, chopped

2 tablespoons J.G. Sweet Reggae Seasoning

1 teaspoon salt

3 chives, chopped

Directions

1. Heat olive oil in a large stock pot over medium heat.
2. Sauté onions and carrots until onion begins to turn translucent, about 3-5 minutes.
3. Add bell peppers and garlic.
4. Continue cooking until garlic is fragrant, about 3 minutes.
5. Add diced tomatoes and chicken broth. Bring to a full boil.
6. Add the remaining ingredients and return to a boil.
7. Reduce heat.
8. Cover and cook for 20 minutes.
9. Serve bowls of shrimp gumbo, garnished with chives or green onions.

Buss-Yu-Belly Stew Peas

Pro Tip: Don't forget!

To make stew peas thicker, take out a cup of the beans and mash them with a fork. If you do not have enough beans, incorporate a 16 ounce can of kidney beans.

Mash to consistency and return to the pot.

Gently stir to combine.

Mash to consistency.....

Buss-Yu-Belly Stew Peas

Ingredients

1 pound packet of red kidney beans
2 pounds of salted pig's tail, cut into 3 inch pieces
1 pound smoked pork neck bones, cut into 3 inches pieces
2 pounds corned beef brisket, cut into 2 inch cubes
1 can coconut milk
1 tablespoon J.G. Jammin' Jerk Seasoning
½ cube chicken boullion
¼ stick butter

Blend together

¼ cup fresh garlic
4 stalks green onions
4 sprigs fresh thyme
4 ounce fresh ginger
1 scotch bonnet pepper (habanero)
¼ cup water

Directions

1. Cook the pig's tail, at a rapid boil for about 10 minutes, to remove excess salt. Discard the water.
2. Taste to check salt level. If it is still too salty, rinse the water again. This may take two or three changes of water until desired saltiness is reached.
3. Place pig's tail, smoked, pork neck bones, beef brisket, and kidney beans in a large pot. Cover with water.
4. Add half of the blended seasonings. Cover pot and simmer for about 1 hour.
5. Test with fork for tenderness.
6. Mix the coconut milk and the remainder of the blended seasoning.
7. Continue cooking on low heat until meats and beans are tender, making sure that the stew is getting thicker.
8. Add J.G. Jammin' Jerk Seasoning, chicken boullion, and ¼ stick butter for last 5 minutes of cooking
9. If more salt is needed, add the remaining chicken bouillon..

Pro Tip: Don't forget!

● Yellow onions have the deepest flavor and are almost inedible while raw, but when applied to heat their flavor and texture changes. This is your all around cooking choice.

○ White onions have a more crunchy and tangy flavor that works for pasta, stir fry or even salsa.

● Sweet onions does have the sweetest flavor and due to the thick layers of onion, it is perfect for broths and especially frying.

● Red onion has the most mild flavor. It is the best either grilled, because it doesn't dry out, or consumed raw in things like guacamole, sandwiches and would be the best choice for pickling.

● Green onion is used mainly as garnish topping and works best with soups, stir fry and even tacos.

Cultural Insight: Stew Peas Wednesday

Stew peas was a weekly Wednesday dinner made by my mother. She would serve it along side white rice seasoned with butter only (no salt), fried ripe plantain and slices of avocado. It is so good that there is no way you would eat one serving of stew peas. You can't help yourself, you just have to go back for more, hence the name 'Bust Yu Belly'.

Our Jamaican cuisine has a sumptuous array of flavors with each of the sixteen parishes (states) cooking the same meals with a different twist to the same recipe. There is no right or wrong way, just a reflection of our many cultural influences.

Jacqui's Succulent Oxtails

Pro Tip: Don't forget!

Don't cut fat from oxtails after seasoning; instead place in baking dish with fat side up. Broil on Hi for 5 minutes on each side or until fat is burned off, then pour off oil and start cooking. When finished cooking, place the pot in the fridge until the oil solidifies. Remove the fat and add butter beans.

Jacqui's Succulent Oxtails

Ingredients

5 pounds oxtails
2 tablespoons J.G. Jammin' Jerk
1 tablespoon beef bouillon
¼ cup coconut oil
1 can (6 ounce) butter beans

Blend together

1 large onion, sliced
4 stalks green onion, cut up
1 scotch bonnet pepper
¼ cup fresh garlic
¼ cup fresh ginger
2 tablespoons Kitchen Bouquet Browning Sauce
½ cup water

Directions

1. In a large bowl season oxtail with J.G. Jammin' Jerk Seasoning, salt, and beef bouillon.
2. Add half of the blended seasonings. Cover and marinate for an hour or overnight (preferred).
3. In a large heavy pot, heat coconut oil and add oxtails turning constantly until browned.
4. Drain the oil add water to cover oxtail. Cover the pot and bring to a rapid boil.
5. Reduce heat and keep adding water a little at a time. Cook until tender about 1½ to 2 hours. Check for tenderness with a fork.
6. Whisk brown gravy and the remainder for seasoning mix. Reduce heat to low and simmer until gravy becomes thick–about 10 minutes.
7. Add butter beans and heat through.

Orange Sauce:

Ingredients

1 cup orange juice

½ cup sugar

2 tablespoons rice vinegar or white vinegar

2 tablespoons soy sauce use tamari for a gluten-free dish

¼ teaspoon ginger

¼ teaspoon garlic powder or 2 garlic cloves, finely diced

½ teaspoon red chili flakes

orange zest from 1 orange

1 tablespoon cornstarch

Garnish

green onions

orange zest

Perfect for chicken shrimp, salmon and stir fried vegetables.

Cultural Insight

Oxtail – aka Waggin' Sirloin: Cowtail (the tail of the cow) had to be pre-ordered from the butcher and the skin of the tail was not removed. This is what gave the cowtail its yummy gumminess. Because of the scarcity of the tail (the cow only has one tail, right?)– you can imagine the demand. The tail had to be ordered in advance, and if you had a good relationship with your butcher, you might even get two tails. Then and only then.

With the demand for cowtail, oxtail was imported to the island, but the oxtail came skinless! The good news is that the Jamaicans adjusted to the lack of skin discovering that the oxtail was just as delicious. Served with rice & peas, and ripe plantain we had a winner.

As a true Jamaican you use your fingers to hold the oxtail in order to get to the meat of the matter, not letting go until the bone is sucked dry.

Wash it down (drink) with a cold glass of carrot juice.

Curry Goat

Pro Tip: Don't forget!

The best parts of the goat to curry are the shank, leg, shoulder, and neck. The bones sustain the long, slow cooking, allowing the succulent flavor to infuse into the meat, creating a rich and tender dish.

Curry Goat

Ingredients

5 pounds mutton (goat)
¼ cup curry powder
2 tablespoons J.G. Jammin' Jerk Seasoning
1 tablespoon chicken bouillon
salt to taste
3 white potatoes, diced

Blend with ½ cup of water

1 large onion
4 stalks green onions
8 ounce fresh ginger, cut up
1 scotch bonnet pepper (or habanero)
4 sprigs fresh thyme
Once these ingredients have been blended, reserve ¼ cup

Directions

1. Season mutton with J.G. Jammin' Jerk Seasoning and ¼ cup of blended seasoning. Allow to marinate for 1 hour or overnight (preferred).
2. In a large pot, heat oil over medium heat until hot.
3. Add the mutton and sauté, stirring frequently. Cover and allow to steam in its own juice for 10 minutes.
4. Add 1 cup of water and simmer until tender (add a little more water as necessary).
5. Add the balance of blended seasonings and potatoes. Simmer on low heat until potatoes are cooked.
6. Taste to see if the pot needs a little more J.G. Jammin' Jerk Seasoning and/or another bouillon cube.

Quick Black Ben and Corn Salad

Ingredients

    2 cans black beans

    1 can whole kernel corn

    1 red onion

    1 red bell paper

    1 avocado

    1 Jalapeño pepper

Dressing

    ½ cup extra-virgin olive oil

    ½ cup lime juice (from about 4 to 6 limes)

    1 cup loosely packed cilantro (mostly leaves, small stems are ok, from about 1 small bunch)

    1 tablespoon honey or maple syrup, to taste

    1 teaspoon Dijon mustard

    ½ teaspoon ground cumin

    Scant ½ teaspoon fine salt, to taste

    1 clove garlic, roughly chopped

Pro Tip: Don't Forget!

Look for a firm but ripe avocado this makes it easy to dice and not mushy.

Cultural Insight: No Goat, No Party

Let the party begin! There is no gathering without curry goat.

Driving along the countryside you will always come across roadside shops that sells Box Goat accompanied by a cup of Manish Water (soup).

Curry goat is served with white rice, boiled green bananas, yellow yam, and roasted breadfruit.

It would be a shame to visit the island of Jamaica and not enjoy a road-side Box Goat. Make sure you drink a Jelly Coconut with a little rum to wash it down.

Crowd Pleasers

Jacqui's Saucy Twist for Any Meal

Jacqui's Saucy Twist for Any Meal

Ingredients

1 bottle J.G. Jammin' Jerk or Sweet Reggae Sauce

1 small can 8 ounce pineapple chunks or mandarin oranges

1 each red, green and yellow bell peppers, thinly sliced

1 small pack mushrooms (optional)

1 tablespoon canola oil

Directions

1. Heat oil in a large skillet over medium-heat.
2. Add bell peppers and mushrooms.
3. Sauté for 2 minutes, then add sauce of your choice and pineapple chunks
4. Bring to boil and simmer on medium for 5 minutes.
5. Pour over your desired meal.

Ackee and Cod Fish

Ackee and Cod Fish

Ingredients

2 cans ackee drained

1 pound cod fish salted pollock

1 onion finely chopped

1 clove garlic, finely chopped

2 stalks green onions, chopped

8 small tomatoes, chopped

2 sprigs thyme

½ scotch bonnet pepper, chopped

¼ cup coconut oil

2 teaspoons J.G. Jammin Jerk Seasoning

6 bacon slices, finely chopped (optional)

1 cup cubed ham (optional)

1 cup cooked smoked turkey leg, cubed (optional)

Directions

1. Place cod fish in a bowl and cover with water. Soak for 2 hours.
2. Use half of salt water with fresh water and bring to boil. Add ackee and boil for 3 minutes. Drain and set aside.
3. Boil cod fish in fresh water for 5 minutes. Drain water. If cod fish is still too salty, rinse again. It may take 1-2 extra rinses, but when the saltiness is to your taste - drain water and flake with a fork.
4. Set aside.
5. In frying pan with oil fry bacon, ham or turkey leg till crisp (only use one). Drain and put aside.
6. Add all seasonings and sauté for 4 minutes. Add cod fish and blend well for 5 minutes.
7. Gently fold the ackee into the cod fish mixture using a spatula. Avoid stirring vigorously to keep the ackee as whole as possible. Just a gentle mixing for flavors to blend. Cover pot and simmer for 5 minutes.
8. Sprinkle J.G. Jammin' Jerk Seasoning and your choice bacon, ham or turkey leg.
9. Serve hot.

Jacqui's Quick Quiche

Ingredients

1 large tortilla

4 eggs

¼ cup cottage cheese

¾ cup shredded cheese

1 cup spinach

1 teaspoon J.G. Jerk Seasoning (optional)

salt and pepper to taste

Directions

1. Place tortilla in round baking dish.
2. Mix eggs, cottage cheese and seasonings in tortilla.
3. Add shredded cheese and spinach.
4. Bake 20 minutes at 200°F.

Cultural Insight

Ackee is the national fruit of Jamaica. Its name is derived from the West African Akye fufo. For a true Jamaican, Sunday isn't Sunday without a delicious breakfast of ackee and saltfish served with the traditional companions of boiled green bananas, slices of fried ripe or green plantains, boiled dumplings, Johnny cakes, festival, breadfruit, or the shallow-fried cassava bread called bammy.

Ackee is best served with hot chocolate (aka cocoa tea), or the world famous Blue Mountain coffee sweetened with condensed milk – altogether a mouth-watering treat!

Tropical Charcuterie Board

Ingredients

8 ounce brie cheese

8 ounce parmesan, thinly sliced

8 ounce smoked gouda

4 ounce bleu cheese

2 ounce cream cheese

½ cup Spanish olives, pitted

½ cup almonds

¼ cup cashews

1 cup strawberries

½ cup blueberries

8 ounce pepperoni

16 ounce salami

8 ounce prosciutto

4 sprigs rosemary

1 cup J.G. Jammin' Jerk Sauce

1 cup J.G. Sweet Reggae Sauce

Directions

1. Arrange all ingredients on a wooden, marble or slate cheese platter.
2. Pour J.G. Jammin' Jerk Sauce and J.G. Sweet Reggae Sauce into small bowls and place between the meats and cheeses.
3. Drizzle sauce over the cream cheese and garnish with rosemary.
4. Enjoy with fresh, crusty baguette and assorted crackers.

Meat, Fowl

and

Seafood

"Way To A Man's Heart..." Pork Chops

Pro Tip: Don't forget!

This recipe also works great with salmon, T-Bone steak, or chicken breasts.

Using flour gives a little crunch to the meat.

"Way To A Man's Heart..." Pork Chops

Ingredients

4 6 ounce center rib pork chops, bone-in thick

Sprinkle with salt to taste

3 teaspoons J.G. Jammin' Jerk Seasoning

1 cube chicken bouillon

2 tablespoons flour

1 tablespoon soy sauce

½ cup pineapple juice

1 cup J.G. Jammin' Jerk Sauce

Directions

1. Season meat with 2 teaspoons J.G. Jammin' Gourmet Jerk Seasoning, chicken bouillon, salt, and soy sauce.

2. In a small bowl, mix flour and 1 teaspoon of J.G. Jammin' Jerk Seasoning.

3. Use paper towel to pat dry the meat then dip in flour mixture on both sides.

4. Heat oil in a medium-sized skillet over medium heat.

5. Add meat and cook until golden brown (2 to 3 minutes on both sides) then reduce heat to low. Cover skillet with lid.

6. Cook for 12 minutes or until thermometer reads 145°F when inserted.

7. Transfer meat to a platter and cover loosely with aluminum foil.

8. Let the meat rest for 5 minutes.

9. While meat rests, pour pineapple juice and J.G. Jammin' Jerk Sauce in skillet and bring to a simmer.

10. Place meat back in the skillet and spoon some J.G. Jammin' Jerk Sauce on top. Simmer on low for 5 minutes.

11. Place in a platter, garnish pork chops with fresh basil and serve.

Jerk Shrimp & Lobster Jamdown

Pro Tip: Don't forget!

Cut the underside of lobster tail down the middle with kitchen scissors or sharp knife. Do not cook lobster beforehand, it will be rubbery.

Jerk Shrimp & Lobster Jamdown

Ingredients

1 pound Argentina red shrimp

4 lobster tails

1 tablespoon J.G. Jammin' Jerk Seasoning

1 cube chicken bouillon

salt to taste

1 tablespoons olive or coconut oil

2 teaspoons fresh thyme, thinly chopped

½ each red, yellow, and green bell pepper, julienned

1 onion, julienned

1 cup J.G. Jammin' Jerk Sauce

Directions

1. Remove uncooked lobster meat from tails.
2. Place lobster and shrimp in bowl, add all dry seasonings. Mix together.
3. Heat oil in a large skillet and add green onions, garlic, and thyme. Sauté for 3 minutes.
4. Add shrimp and lobster. Sauté for 10 minutes.
5. Add J.G. Jammin' Jerk Sauce, onions and bell peppers.
6. Simmer for 5 minutes.

Mouthwatering Jerk Rib Eye Steak

Pro Tip: Don't forget!

If in a hurry and you do not have the time to refrigerate, season and let the steak rest at room temperature for 30 minutes before cooking.

Tilt skillet from side to side make sure that skillet is well coated with oil and butter.

Mouthwatering Jerk Rib Eye Steak

Ingredients

2 1¼ pound bone-in ribeye steak

2 teaspoons J.G. Jammin' Jerk Seasoning

½ teaspoon salt

2 tablespoons butter

2 tablespoons olive oil

1 cup J.G. Jammin' Jerk Sauce

Directions

1. Place rib eye steak onto a sheet pan and sprinkle J.G. Jammin' Jerk Seasoning and salt on both sides of steak, making sure to rub it into the steak so that it sticks.

2. Cover steaks and let them rest in the refrigerator for 1 hour or overnight (preferred).

3. Remove from refrigerator and allow to rest at room temperature for 30 minutes before cooking.

4. Heat skillet over medium heat before adding butter and olive oil to skillet.

5. Carefully add steaks to hot skillet and cook on both sides for 3 minutes, basting with butter and oil constantly.

6. Add J.G. Jammin' Jerk Sauce to steak and keep basting with the J.G. Jammin' Jerk Sauce, oil and butter until dark brown and caramelized on both sides for 2 minutes.

7. Remove from skillet to serving platter. Let rest for 5 minutes before serving.

Pro Tip: Don't Forget

Cooking Steak

Rare - 1 min each side

Medium Rare - 2 mins each side

Medium - 3 mins each side

Medium Well - 4 mins each side

Well - 5 mins each side

Jacqui's Lovable Lamb Chops

Jacqui's Lovable Lamb Chops

Ingredients

6 lamb chops

¼ cup extra virgin oil

2 tablespoons J.G. Jammin' Jerk Seasoning

kosher salt to taste

1 cup J.G. Jammin' Jerk Sauce

Directions

1. In a large bowl, mix the oil, J.G. Jammin' Jerk Seasoning and salt. Rub on both sides of lamb shops.
2. Place in a ziploc bag and marinate for 1 hour in the refrigerator.
3. Remove from the refrigerator and allow the chops to come to room temperature (about 30 minutes).
4. Heat grill to 350°F or heat oil in cast iron pan.
5. Add lamb chops and sear for 2 minutes on each side.
6. Move lamb chops to indirect heat and brush on J.G. Jammin' Jerk Sauce.
7. Continue to cook for 3 minutes more for medium rare, or 4 minutes more for medium.
8. Let chop rest for about 5 minutes.
9. Garnish with chopped fresh rosemary.

Pro Tip: Don't Forget

Always cook chicken until it is no longer pink in the center. Pierce chicken with a fork or thermometer – reading should be above 165°F and the juice should run clear.

If using a grill with coals, make sure coals are white before adding the chicken.

Jacqui's Jammin' Jerk Chicken

Jacqui's Jammin' Jerk Chicken

Ingredients

Preheat oven to 375°F

2 whole chickens cut in quarters (your butcher will cut the chicken in quarters for you)

4 tablespoons J.G. Jammin' Jerk Seasoning

1 teaspoon salt

1 tablespoon oil

¼ cup soy sauce

2 limes, cut in half

Directions

1. Rub lime on chicken, rinse and pat dry. Combine all ingredients in a small bowl.
2. Mix all dry ingredients with oil.
3. Rub seasoning mix on both sides of chicken and place in a large bowl.
4. Cover and refrigerate for 1 hour or overnight (preferred)

Oven Directions

1. Place chicken in a greased roasting pan and bake for 40-45 minutes.
2. Allow to cool for 5 minutes.
3. Brush chicken with J.G. Jammin' Jerk Sauce on both sides and place under the broiler for 5 minutes for desired color.

Grill Directions

1. Place chicken on grill turning frequently for 40 minutes.
2. Brush J.G. Jammin' Jerk Sauce on both sides and continue grilling for 10 minutes.
3. Cover chicken loosely with foil and allow to rest for 5 minutes.

Jamaican Jerk Marinade

Ingredients

1 large yellow onion

1 bunch green onions

2 bulb garlic

1 thumb of ginger

1 bunch fresh thyme

2 tablespoons white vinegar

2 tablespoons vegetable oil

1 fresh orange squeezed or ¼ cup orange juice

Add ¼ fresh orange peel to the blender

2 tablespoons of browning or molasses for color

5 tablespoons J.G. Jammin' Jerk Seasoning

5 scotch bonnet peppers, 2 green, 3 ripe. Leave green ones whole and remove seeds from ripened peppers for a mild marinade. Leave all seeds and membranes in for more spice. Add more salt if you want it more salty

Blend all the ingredients in a food processor or a blender. If you want it less liquid, then reduce oil and vinegar amounts. Use to marinate your meat overnight. Store in refrigerator for up to 12 months.

Cultural Insight

Street food is our go-to for quick, inexpensive and delicious food. Take Pan Chicken for example, with the exciting smell of the smoke produced while cooking will make you salivate as you wait to be served!

Jacqui's Fall-Off-The Bone Jerk Ribs

Ingredients

2 racks baby back ribs

¼ cup J.G. Jammin' Jerk Seasoning

½ teaspoon salt

4 cubes chicken bouillon

1 12-ounce can of beer or 2 cups orange juice

1 bottle J.G. Jammin' Jerk Sauce

A few drops of Kitchen Bouquet Browning & Seasoning Sauce

Directions

1. Combine all dry ingredients plus Kitchen Bouquet Browning Sauce in a small bowl and rub on both sides of ribs. Cover and refrigerate for 1 hour or overnight.
2. Spray roasting pan with cooking oil, e.g. Pam.
3. Add ribs to pan and pour beer or orange juice over ribs. Cover with foil and tightly seal.
4. Bake at 350°F for 2 hours or until tender.
5. Remove the ribs from the pan and place on a platter.
6. Pour liquid from roasting pan into saucepan and bring to boil.
7. Lower heat to a simmer and cook until reduced by half or about one cup.
8. Brush J.G. Jammin' Jerk Sauce on both sides of ribs.
9. Broil in oven for 5 minutes on both sides until browned or slightly charred.
10. Remove and let ribs rest for 5 minutes.
11. Cut between the bones and place on platter.
12. Pour the remaining sauce on ribs.

Jacqui's Hack:
Quick Reggae Ribs

Ingredients

Preheat oven to 375°F unless you are using the grill

2 racks pre-cooked unseasoned ribs from your local supermarket

¼ cup pineapple juice or orange juice

4 tablespoons J.G. Jammin' Jerk Seasoning

1 cup J.G. Jammin' Jerk Sauce

Directions

1. Sprinkle J.G. Jammin' Jerk Seasoning generously on both sides.
2. Add orange or pineapple juice.
3. Place in roasting pan and cover with oil.
4. Place in preheated oven for 10 minutes or grill on medium high for 10 minutes.
5. Open foil and brush on a generous amount of J.G. Jammin' Jerk Sauce.
6. Return to grill, or oven for 5 minutes on both sides or until browned or slightly charred.
7. Let ribs rest for 5 minutes.
8. Cut between the bones, place on platter and pour on more J.G. Jammin' Jerk Sauce!

Jacqui's Hack:
Quick Jerk Chicken

Ingredients

Preheat oven to 375°F (unless you are using the grill)

2 racks pre-cooked chicken from your local supermarket

¼ cup pineapple or orange juice

2 tablespoons J.G. Jammin' Jerk Seasoning

1 cup J.G. Jammin' Jerk Sauce

Directions

1. Sprinkle J.G. Jammin' Jerk Seasoning generously on both sides.
2. Add ¼ cup orange or pineapple juice. Place in roasting pan and cover with foil.
3. Place in oven for 10 minutes, or grill on medium-high for 10 minutes.
4. Open foil and brush on a generous amount of J.G. Jammin' Jerk Sauce.
5. Return to grill or oven for 5 minutes on both sides, or until browned or slightly charred.
6. Let chicken rest for 5 minutes.
7. Cut between the bones.
8. Place on platter and pour on more J.G. Jammin' Jerk Sauce!

Jammin' Salmon

Jammin' Salmon

Ingredients

Preheat oven to 400°F

1 salmon fillet (approximately 2 pounds)

¼ cup olive oil

2½ tablespoons J.G. Jammin' Jerk Seasoning

½ teaspoon salt

1 cup J.G. Jammin' Jerk Sauce

1 small can of 8 ounce pineapple chunks

Marinade

1. Combine olive oil, J.G. Jammin' Jerk Seasoning, and salt in a bowl and rub on salmon.
2. Marinade for an hour in the fridge.

Sauce

1. In saucepan, add J.G. Jammin' Jerk Sauce and pineapple chunks and bring to boil for 5 minutes then set aside.
2. Wrap salmon tightly in foil and place on a baking sheet in preheated oven at 400°F.
3. Bake for 10 minutes.
4. Remove salmon from oven and open foil to pour J.G. Jammin' Jerk Sauce over the salmon.
5. Broil or grill on low for 5 minutes to get a crispy golden charred edge.
6. Let rest for 5 minutes then place on platter and garnish with lemon.

Jacqui's Piquant Jerk Wings

Jacqui's Piquant Jerk Wings

Ingredients

3 pounds fresh chicken wings

¼ cup olive oil

1 teaspoon kosher salt

2 tablespoons J.G. Jammin' Jerk Seasoning

1 cup J.G. Jammin' Jerk Sauce

Directions

1. In a large bowl stir together all ingredients and coat wings.
2. Place evenly on greased baking sheet.
3. Bake in oven or grill (with lid closed) at 350°F for 30 minutes, turning once or twice.
4. Move wings to indirect heat and brush J.G. Jammin' Jerk Sauce on all sides.
5. Continue to grill with lid closed for 10 to 15 minutes. If using the oven, broil for 5-10 minutes.

We Jammin' Jerk Burger

Ingredients

4¾ inch thick hamburger meat (80% lean 20% fat)

J.G. Jammin' Jerk Seasoning

salt to taste

Toppings

4 slices provolone cheese

dill pickle slices

fresh red onions

large tomato slices

green leaf or iceberg lettuce

pineapple slices (optional)

J.G. Jammin' Jerk Sauce

brioche, classic sesame seed or potato buns

Directions

1. Season burger with salt and a generous amount of J.G. Jammin' Jerk Seasoning on both sides.
2. Preheat grill to medium-heat. Set oven to broil.
3. Cook burger patties covered for 3-5 minutes each side—until internal temperature reaches 160°F.
4. Flip burger patties when juices are accumulating on top of burger and you have a good sear.
5. Top with cheese and return to heat for no more than 1 minute to allow cheese to melt.
6. Slice and prepare all burger toppings.
7. Cut buns in half and spread with softened butter. Toast the cut side on a skillet or grill until golden brown.
8. Pour a generous amount of J.G. Jammin' Jerk Sauce on both buns.
9. Build your burger!

Breaded Lamb Chops

Breaded Lamb Chops

Ingredients

1 small rack of lamb (about 1¾ pounds)

1 tablespoon J.G. Jammin Jerk Seasoning

1 cup Panko Japanese Style Breadcrumbs

1 egg, beaten

2 tablespoon parmesan cheese, finely shredded

¼ cup olive oil

salt and pepper to taste

Directions

1. Trim excess fat from the rack of lamb and cut it into 8 individual chops.
2. Season chops on both sides with salt and pepper and set aside.
3. In a shallow bowl, lightly beat one egg and set aside.
4. On a plate, toss 1 cup of Panko Japanese Breadcrumbs with parmesan.
5. Dip lamb chops in the egg wash and evenly coat with the seasoned breadcrumbs by pressing each chop's sides into the mixture.
6. Heat oil in a large nonstick skillet over medium heat.
7. Add chops and occasionally flip until golden brown and cooked through (approximately 4 minutes on each side).
8. Arrange on a platter and serve with warm J.G. Jammin Jerk Sauce.

Jerk Chicken Tortilla

Jerk Chicken Tortilla

Ingredients

2 tablespoons J.G. Jammin' Jerk Seasoning

kosher salt to taste

1½ pounds boneless, skinless chicken thighs

1 tablespoon coconut oil

12 mini flour tortillas, warmed

1 cup pico de gallo

1 ripe avocado halved, peeled, seeded and diced

½ cup chopped fresh cilantro leaves

½ cup J.G. Jammin' Jerk Sauce

Directions

1. In a small bowl season chicken with J.G. Jammin' Jerk Seasoning and salt.
2. Heat oil in a large skillet over medium high heat.
3. Add chicken to the skillet in a single layer and cook until golden brown for 5 minutes on both sides or reaching 165°F internal temperature.
4. Let chicken rest for 5 minutes before dicing into bite-sized pieces.
5. Serve chicken in tortilla, topped with pico de gallo, avocado and cilantro.
6. Drizzle with J.G. Jammin' Jerk Sauce.

Moreish
Side Dishes

Festival Rice

Festival Rice

Ingredients

1 16 ounce can whole kernel corn

2 cups Jasmine rice

2 cups water

½ cup coconut milk

1 envelope Goya Ham Flavored Concentrate

2 tablespoon J.G. Sweet Reggae Seasoning

1 cube chicken bouillon

1 teaspoon salt

2 tablespoon butter

1 each red and green bell peppers, cut up into small chunks

Directions

1. In a medium pot add corn, water, coconut milk, J.G. Sweet Reggae Seasoning, Goya Ham Flavored Concentrate, and butter.
2. Bring to boil.
3. Add rice and cover pot.
4. Simmer rice for 15 to 20 minutes, stirring once.
5. Remove from heat.
6. Add bell peppers and fluff rice.
7. Let stand for 5 minutes before serving.

Jacqui's Jamdown Rice & Peas

Jacqui's Jamdown Rice & Peas

Ingredients

1 can green pigeon peas or red kidney beans
2 cups water
½ cup coconut milk
2 cups Jasmine rice
2 tablespoon J.G. Jammin' Jerk Seasoning
1 teaspoon salt
1 tablespoon coconut oil or butter

Directions

1. In a medium pot add peas, water, coconut milk, J.G. Jammin' Jerk Seasoning and salt.
2. Bring to a full boil.
3. Stir in rice, and cover pot.
4. Lower heat to simmer and cook for 15 to 20 minutes, stirring once.
5. Remove from heat and let stand for five minutes.
6. Fluff rice with fork.

Tip to cook the perfect rice

Use cold water, to rinse rice thoroughly in a fine-mesh sieve/ strainer until water runs clear. This removes excess starch from the rice, which will make it gummy.

For Long - grain white rice

1 cup
2 cups water
1 tablespoon butter
salt to taste
Cook for 18 minutes on low heat

Short - grain white rice

1 cup
1 ¼ cups water
1 tablespoon butter
salt to taste
Cook for 15 minutes on low heat

Brown rice

1 cup
1 ¾ cups water
1 tablespoon butter
salt to taste
Cook for 45 minutes on low heat

Pro Tip: Don't Forget

Fluff rice with fork and let rest for 5 to 10 minutes.

Cultural Insight:
Traditional Jamaican Sunday Dinner

Any Jamaican will tell you that Sunday dinner must be accompanied by rice & peas. Quite simply this is non-negotiable.

Although the most common type of rice & peas in Jamaica is actually made with red kidney beans, the dish Jamaican should never ever be referred to as "rice and beans" or "peas and rice". There is no other phrase that will forever mark you as a non-Jamaican as one of those two.

So, if you want to embrace the culture, please help yourself to a delicious serving of "rice and peas".

Jacqui's Ultimate Mac & Cheese

Jacqui's Ultimate Mac & Cheese

Ingredients

1 16 ounce pack large elbow macaroni

¼ cup oil

2 cups heavy whipping cream

2 cups milk

8 ounce butter

1 tablespoon J.G. Sweet Reggae seasoning

½ teaspoon salt

1 tablespoon corn starch

4 cups sharp Cheddar cheese, shredded

1 cup smoked Gouda cheese, shredded

3 large eggs

1 large onion

1 cup milk

4 ounce butter melted

1 cup Panko Japanese Style Breadcrumbs

Mix together well. Put aside.

Directions

1. Cook pasta according to instructions on the package, adding a tablespoon of oil.
2. Remove from heat. Drain in colander under cold water. Let drain and put in large bowl. Set aside to cool
3. Using blender, blend eggs, onion and milk until smooth. Pour over cool pasta. Mix well and set aside
4. In a stock pot, combine heavy cream, butter and milk. Whisk in J.G. Sweet Reggae Seasoning, salt and cornstarch. Bring to a boil while whisking continuously. Once it reaches a boil, add the cheese and continue to whisk until the sauce is smooth.
5. Add the pasta and mix together.
6. Transfer to a greased baking dish. Sprinkle with breadcrumbs evenly on top and bake for 45 minutes.

Zesty Orange Cornbread

Zesty Orange Cornbread

Ingredients

4 boxes Jiffy cornbread mix

1 16 ounce tub of sour cream

1 16 ounce can of whole kernel corn

4 eggs

2 tablespoon vegetable oil

1 teaspoon orange extract

½ teaspoon cinnamon

½ stick of butter

Directions

1. Preheat oven to 400°F
2. Combine all ingredients and place in a greased 9" x 12" baking dish.
3. Bake for 45 minutes, or until golden brown; rub butter on top of cornbread during the last five minutes of baking.
4. Rest for 10 minutes before serving.

Drunk Plantain

Cultural Insight:

There is never a meal without plantains as it adds sweetness to our savory meals.

Drunk Plantain

Ingredients

Preheat oven to 350°F

6 ripe plantains (black with a little yellow)

2 cups vegetable oil

Sauce

2 cups orange or pineapple juice

½ cup brown sugar

1 tablespoon cinnamon powder

¼ teaspoon salt

1 tablespoon corn starch

¼ cup amaretto liquor

In sauce pot bring to boil whisking until thickened about 5 minutes. Set aside.

Directions

1. Cut the ends of each plantains and score the skin from top to bottom (do not cut through the plantains).
2. Slice the plantain on an angle to make longer pieces about ⅓ inches thick.
3. Preheat oil in a large deep skillet over medium heat.
4. Fry the pieces until golden brown. Place on paper towel to drain excess oil.
5. Arrange in a greased baking pan and pour sauce over plantains (make sure that sauce covers plantains evenly).
6. Bake for 30 minutes.
7. Arrange on a platter.

Variations of Cheesecake

Basic Cheesecake Recipe

Ingredients

Crust

1½ Graham Cracker crumbs

2 tablespoon brown or white sugar

pinch of salt

7 tablespoon melted butter

Filling

2 pounds cream cheese

2 tablespoon flour

5 (room temperature) eggs

⅔ cup sour Cream

1 cup white sugar

⅛ tablespoon salt

1½ tablespoon vanilla

Directions

1. Prepare the oven and pan:
   Preheat oven to 325°F. Position a rack in the middle of the oven.

2. Make the crust:
   - Place the butter in a medium microwave-safe bowl. Cover the bowl with a paper towel and microwave in 10-second increments until melted.
   - Brush the bottom and sides of a 9-inch springform pan with a small amount of the melted butter.
   - In the bowl with the remaining melted butter, mix the graham cracker crumbs, sugar, and salt until well combined.
   - Press the crumb mixture evenly into the bottom of the prepared pan. Ensure it is well-packed and reaches the edges.
   - Bake the crust in the preheated oven until golden brown, about 15-18 minutes. Remove from the oven and let cool.
   - Wrap the outside of the springform pan with a large piece of foil, covering the bottom and sides, to make it waterproof. Place the pan in a roasting pan.

3. Prepare the cheesecake filling:
 - In a large bowl, beat the softened cream cheese and sugar together with an electric mixer on medium speed until smooth, about 1 minute.
 - Add the sour cream and vanilla extract. Mix on low speed until just combined.
 - Add the eggs one at a time, mixing gently by hand until just combined. Avoid over mixing to prevent the cheesecake from puffing up and cracking.

4. Bake the cheesecake:
 - Pour the cheesecake batter evenly over the cooled crust, smoothing the top.
 - Carefully pour hot water into the roasting pan, filling it to come halfway up the sides of the foil-wrapped springform pan, creating a water bath.
 - Bake the cheesecake in the preheated oven until the edges are set but the center is still slightly jiggly, about 1 hour and 20 minutes.

5. Cool the cheesecake:
 - Turn off the oven and leave the cheesecake inside with the door slightly ajar for 1 hour.
 - Remove the cheesecake from the water bath and place it on a cooling rack. Run a knife around the edge to loosen it from the pan.
 - Allow the cheesecake to cool to room temperature. Cover and refrigerate for at least 8 hours or overnight before serving.

6. Serve:
 - When ready to serve, run a knife around the edge of the pan once more and unlock to unmold the cheesecake. Transfer to a serving platter or cake stand and smooth the edges with a knife.

Mango

Ingredients

Basic Cheesecake mixture

1½ cups mango puree and bits and some slices for decoration

2 tablespoons lemon juice

whipped cream for the top

*Mango Glaze (recipe follows)

Directions

1. Fold in ½ cup mango puree and bits into the Basic Cheesecake mixture along with lemon juice.
2. To bake follow the directions for Basic Cheesecake. Spread the mango glaze on top. Decorate with whipped cream and mango slices.

Mango Glaze

Ingredients

1 cup mango puree

⅓ cup sugar

½ cup water

2 tablespoons cornstarch

1 tablespoon lemon juice

Directions

1. Mix all ingredients together in a saucepan. Bring to a boil then lower heat and keep stirring until it thickens. Cool and spread on the cheesecake.

Pineapple Cheesecake

Ingredients

1½ cups of crushed pineapple (canned or fresh pineapple can be used)

2 tablespoon white rum (optional)

toasted coconut (optional)

cherries (optional for decorating)

Directions

1. Add ½ cup crushed pineapple and rum to Basic Cheesecake Mixture.
2. Bake as directed
3. Cool. Finish with pineapple glaze, whipped cream and cherries.

Pineapple Glaze

Ingredients

1 cup crushed pineapple

½ cup granulated sugar

½ cup water

2 tablespoons cornstarch

1 tablespoon vanilla

1 tablespoon white rum

Directions

1. Mix all ingredients together in a saucepan. Bring to a boil then lower heat and keep stirring until it thickens. Cool and spread on the cheesecake.

Guava

Ingredients

1 cup Guava puree
1 tablespoon Lime or Lemon rind

Directions

1. Fold in ½ cup puree to Basic Cheesecake Mixture.
2. Bake as per instructions for Basic Cheesecake.
3. When cooled spread remaining glaze on top and border with whip cream.

Desserts

Sweet Life Bread Custard

Sweet Life Bread Custard

Ingredients

Preheat oven to 350°F

1 large loaf of white sliced bread

1 stick butter, melted

1 cup cranberries

cinnamon powder for sprinkling

2 cups heavy whipping cream

2 cups milk

12 eggs

2 teaspoons vanilla

1 teaspoon salt

1½ cup sugar

½ cup port wine

¼ cup white or gold rum (optional)

Directions

1. Grease medium sized foil pan with butter. Place 6 slices of bread at the bottom of the pan and drizzle butter over the bread.
2. Sprinkle cinnamon powder on top. Add a handful of cranberries
3. Add another layer of bread with butter and cinnamon
4. Repeat layers, alternating bread with cranberries until there are 4-5 layers, ending with a top layer of bread, sprinkled with cinnamon. Set aside.
5. Mix together cream, milk, eggs, vanilla, salt, sugar, wine and rum (optional).
6. Pour over bread and let stand for half an hour. Bake for 1 hour
7. Allow to cool down in refrigerator for 1 hour.
8. Place serving platter on top and turn pudding over.
9. Garnish with strawberries and blueberries and serve with warm Rum Sauce.

Brie Cheese in Puff Pastry

Ingredients

- 1 sheet of puff pastry, thawed in the fridge
- 1 small round Brie cheese
- 2 teaspoons brown sugar
- ½ chopped pecans
- honey or agave
- 1 egg beaten

Directions

1. Roll out puff pastry to fit 12 x 12 baking dish.
2. Place sugar, pecans and drizzle honey or agave on top to moisten.
3. Pull up puff pastry and fold into a knot on top.
4. Brush with egg.
5. Bake at 350°F for 20 - 25 minutes or until golden. Serve with crackers.

Cultural Insight: Bread Puddin'

Jamaicans are some of the most industrious and resourceful people on the planet. They don't let anything go to waste–especially not day-old bread.

This generations-old dessert (dubbed bread puddin') is typically made with day-old Hardo bread. And, just as the name suggests, Hardo bread has a dense, chewy texture that is easily devoured in one sitting with nothing, but butter generously spread on top.

The famous Coronation Bakery located in Port Antonio is known to have the best Hardo bread on the island.

Jamaicans are famous for taking any left-over bread (meaning, you may need to hide it from the family to ensure there are leftovers) and making a rich, satisfying dessert that can be served with the traditional Sunday dinner.

Rum Sauce

Rum Sauce

Ingredients

    1 cup heavy whipping cream

    ½ cup sugar

    ¼ teaspoon salt

    1 tablespoon vanilla

    ¼ cup gold or white rum

Directions

1. Bring the cream, sugar, salt, vanilla and rum to a boil. Keep whisking while simmering on low heat for 5 minutes.
2. Mix 1½ teaspoons corn starch to 1 tablespoon of water. Add to mixture and whisk into mixture for 1 minute.
3. Turn off heat and allow to rest for 5 minutes.
4. Pour into bowl. Serve warm.

Tropical Ambrosia

Tropical Ambrosia

Ingredients

1 16 ounce can pineapple chunks (drained)

1 16 ounce can mandarin orange segments (drained)

1 large ripe mango (cut into bite-sized chunks)

1 cup mini marshmallows

1 cup shredded coconut

1 cup maraschino cherries (drained and halved)

2 cups whipped topping

Directions

1. Combine all the ingredients in a large bowl and refrigerate for at least an hour before serving.

Thirst Quenches

Chef's Note:

Sorrel – the Jamaican word for hibiscus – is a beloved, festive drink made from the drying of the hibiscus flower which grows abundantly on the island.

This drink is usually served during the holidays but can be enjoyed over ice any time of the year.

Typically mixed with cloves, all spice, fresh ginger and a splash (or two) of rum, this drink makes for a tropical delight that is both refreshing, warming on the inside and often served when friends and family gather together.

Sorrel Sangria

Sorrel Sangria

Ingredients

8 ounce sorrel (hibiscus flowers)

1 gallon of spring water

4 ounce fresh ginger blended (using 1 cup of water from the gallon)

8 ounce granulated sugar

1 cup port wine

1 cup white rum (optional)

1 cup pineapple chunks

1 cup peaches, chopped into bite-sized chunks

1 cup nectarines, chopped into bite-sized chunks

Directions

1. Bring water to a rapid boil.
2. Stir in sorrel and ginger and boil for 10 minutes.
3. Cover and leave overnight.
4. Strain sorrel into a bowl. Add sugar and wine.
5. Strain again before pouring into serving pitcher.
6. Garnish pitcher with thinly sliced oranges, pineapple, peaches and nectarines.
7. Serve with ice.

Pro Tip:

The University of the West Indies at Mona in Kingston, Jamaica has estimated that there are some 3,000 species of fruits and vegetables on the island. And being the naturally resourceful people that they are, Jamaicans have found a use for every single one!

Whether it's for a refreshing tropical beverage, to soothe a sore throat, or calm an upset stomach, Jamaicans have determined what each plant is good for and have utilized it to the maximum.

**Mango and Guava
Tropical Delight**

Mango and Guava Tropical Delight

Ingredients

3 large very ripe mangoes

1 dozen ripe guavas

4 ounce of fresh ginger

1 gallon bottle of spring water

1½ cup sugar (adjust to taste)

½ cup lemon or lime juice

Directions

1. Put mangoes, guavas and ginger in blender with enough water to cover the fruits and blend.
2. Strain fruit juice and pour into a pitcher. Add remaining water.
3. Add sugar and lemon juice.
4. Serve over ice.

Carrot Juice

Chef's Note:

This drink is a must with Sunday dinner, or something is missing!

Carrot Juice

Ingredients

2 pounds carrots, peeled and washed

4 cups water

1 can condensed milk

1 teaspoon nutmeg

pinch of salt

2 teaspoons vanilla

¼ cup white rum

¼ cup port wine

Directions

1. Using a juicer, juice the carrots.
2. Transfer to blender and add the condensed milk, vanilla, nutmeg and salt.
3. Blend until smooth.
4. Serve cold with ice.

Rum Punch

Pro Tip:

In America we are not always able to find the strawberry syrup that is normally used to color this beverage. But don't worry, this version of the popular drink is every bit as inviting as it is delicious.

Rum Punch

Ingredients

2½ cups pineapple juice

2½ cups orange juice

1 cup Wray & Nephew White Rum

½ cup dark rum

½ cup coconut rum

⅓ cup fresh squeezed lime juice (or 4 limes)

3 tablespoons grenadine

Directions

1. In a pitcher, combine and stir all ingredients.
2. Serve over ice.

WINE PAIRINGS
for
JACQUI'S RECIPES

Generally speaking, J.G. Sauces and Seasonings—a complex blend of spices—beg for a wine with a lot of body to counteract the rich flavors.

Wines such as Tempranillo and Zinfandel are great options. Malbec is well regarded as BBQ's best friend worldwide and will enhance smoky flavors. A standard guideline I use is that the more decadent the preparation of the meat, the more richness, color, and tannin I can have in my choice of wine. I match the depth of the dish with the intensity of the wine.

Pinot Noir and dry Rosé pair well with robust dishes. Sometimes, Rosé wines are a better option than white or red unless the sauce or prepared dish is inherently sweet. And if you're strictly a white wine drinker, Sauvignon Blanc would be a suitable choice for many of the dishes contained in Nyam Thyme.

Jammin' Jerk Sauce

Don't Worry Be A Healthy Jerk!

The health benefits from ingredients that make Jerk:

Scotch Bonnet Pepper

- The scotch bonnet pepper is a variety of chili pepper similar to, and of, the same species as the habanera.
- Has a unique and slightly apricot-like flavor which is delightful assuming the tongue can discern it beyond the intense heat.
- Has the highest concentration of capsicum.
- Spicing up your life with hot pepper can help turn the tables on diabetes.

New evidence shows capsaicin makes your cells more sensitive to insulin and improve the balance between blood sugar and insulin in your body.

Green Onion (Scallion)

Can be used as a tea to relieve cold and fever.

Garlic

A natural antibiotic. Used raw it relieves symptoms of influenza, hypertension, infections and skin conditions.

Ginger

Protects your heart and is good for stomachaches. Calms the stomach, stops the sensation of nausea and accelerates the digestive process. Helps constipation, diarrhea and arthritis.

Pimento (Allspice)

Revs immunity system. Antibacterial and anti-inflammatory that has been proven to kill germs.

Coconut Oil

Packed with Laurie acid. Proven to reduce cholesterol and balance blood sugar levels.

Nutmeg

Aids in digestion, liver and skin problems.

Cinnamon

Spice up blood sugar control. Helps with high cholesterol. Packed with antioxidants and loaded with manganese. Cinnamon tea is used to soothe nerves, upset stomach, relieve cold and flu symptoms.

Tomato

Controls blood pressure. Scrubs arteries clean. Sauces made with tomatoes (BBQ) and ketchup helps keep brittle bones at bay.

Thyme

Ideal for calming nerves, alleviating indigestion and cleaning the mucous membranes.

Vinegar

Improves insulin sensitivity before a high carbohydrate meal. It inhibits the breakdown of carbohydrates, thereby decreasing blood glucose spikes.

Sweet Reggae Sauce

"OUT OF MANY HERBS ONE EXOTIC SEASONING"

- No HEAT Just Sweet!

A reflection of our motto, "Out of Many, One People." Jamaican cuisine is the product of a wide range of culinary influences, that of the Chinese, Dutch, French, Indians, English, Irish, Syrians, Germans and many more. They brought their own distinctive ingredients and flavors. Some Jamaican dishes are spicy and some are sweet. There is a big difference between the two. The real secret of achieving the correct depth of flavors which include mixtures of tanginess and cool sweetness of its many tropical herbs and fruits is found in this sauce and seasoning.

Onions

Contain high levels of quercetin, an antioxidant that has powerful anti-inflammatory effects. Add onions to your meal every day.

Bell Pepper (Any color)

Rich in lutein as well as vitamin C, an antioxidant that may help reduce the risk for cataracts and macular degeneration by protecting cells from damage caused by free radicals.

Thyme

Ideal for calming nerves, alleviating indigestion and clearing the mucous membranes.

Vinegar

Mix ⅛ cup vinegar with ¼ cup water and drink before a high carbohydrate meal. Improves insulin sensitivity. It inhibits the breakdown of carbohydrates, thereby decreasing spikes in blood glucose.

Curry

Keeps your brain sharp. Stops the pain and swelling of rheumatoid arthritis by blocking joint inflammation. Battles high blood pressure and maintains sharp eyesight.

Basil

Relieves fever, indigestion, anxiety and insomnia.

Oregano

Remedy for respiratory tract infection. Relieves indigestion.

Lime

Citrus fruits are famous for containing Vitamin C which helps cold and flu by boosting your immunity. Helps your vision and prevents heart and stroke through fighting inflammation. Also important in keeping your teeth and gums healthy.

Parsley

High Vitamin C content. Prevents inflammatory polyarthritis and good for rheumatoid arthritis.

Olive Oil

Contains the most natural antioxidants to improve cholesterol. Brings down high blood pressure, clears away blood clots. The high content of phenolic compounds in virgin olive oil primes your body to prevent blood clots. Keeps blood flowing more smoothly and lowers your risk of heart attack or stroke.

Cultural Insight: JaMex Cuisine

The motto of Jamaica is, "Out of Many One People" due to the island's rich diversity of ethnicities.

In recent times, Kingston's vibrant restaurant scene has become more and more inclusive of new cultures that weren't necessarily indigenous to the island but surely make for a wicked new fusion of flavors.

Dubbed "JaMex", the combination of Jamaican and Mexican cuisines, has fascinated locals for the past few years when the first JaMex restaurant opened on Hope Road, just a short distance from the Bob Marley Museum located in Kingston.

Cultural Insight: Port Royal

Port Royal is a village located at the mouth of Kingston Harbour founded in 1494 by the Spanish: it was once the largest city in the Caribbean, functioning as the center of shipping and commerce in the Caribbean Sea!

With a new cruise ship port, the historic Port Royal is one of the gateways to the gastronomic city of Kingston. Its waters are an archaeological gold mine, filled with pieces dating back to the 17th century. It's a tight-knit, laidback community of proud Jamaicans.

Peep into yesteryears with a stop at Giddy House, a former artillery store, sunk and tilted by the 1907 earthquake.

Enjoy the catch of the day at any of the local restaurants. Just writing about the catch of the day brings memories of fresh steam, fried, roast or brown stew fish, curry crab, lobster and shrimp, hot flavorful fish tea. Rocking to the beat of reggae music, with a Red Stripe Beer, Ting Soda, Ginger Beer (a non-alcoholic beverage) or another beverage of choice in hand, hanging with the locals and having a good time.

Then jump on a boat for a 15 minutes journey to Lime Key to enjoy swimming in the crystal water and socializing with friends.

A VISIT TO JAMAICA

A must go is Kingston where I am from to feel the rhythm of Jamaica

The Jamaica Tourist Board says this about Kingston

"It's a one -of- a- kind, half exotic jungle bursting with sunshine, part thriving business district, and full of uniquely Jamaican lifestyle. With plenty to see and do. Kingston is a crash course in life on the island.

The beat of Reggae. The searing smell of Jerk over the fire. The swizzle of rum in your glass.

No place on earth provides the range of attractions and the cultural diversity that can be found here. No place on earth feels like it. No place on earth sounds like it."

Jamaica Heartbeat of the World.

Visit their website www.visitjamaica.com for planning your vacation

Note:

One worthwhile piece of advice I would like to share is that when planning your trip to Jamaica please ensure you are using a tour guide approved by the Jamaica Tourist Board.

Jamaica has a rich history in Track and Field producing the Fastest Sprinters in the world. Jamaicans have speediness in their genes because of the food.

Reggae music originated in Jamaica in the late 1960s and was largely made popular worldwide by the late musical legend Bob Marley.

Nearly four decades after his passing, Bob Marley has consistently ranked among the top 10 highest-earning deceased celebrities for the past five years.

Peppa Thyme

RESTAURANT & BAR

A must-go for me

An oasis that provides a beautiful, rustic green space with excellent food. Once you enter, the tantalizing aroma of jerk instantly makes your mouth water!

The swizzle of rum, whether in your glass or drizzled over your jerk ribs, is that essential touch that makes them irresistibly finger-licking good.

Go to their website to book your table.

www.peppathymejm.com

The Origins of Jerk

Jerk is a style of cooking native to Jamaica, in which meat is dry-rubbed or wet marinated with a hot spice mixture called Jamaican Jerk Spice. It was originally developed by the Maroons, a group of Africans inhabiting the densely forested mountains of Jamaica who lived independently and maintained their rich African heritage through food, dance, music, and religion while keeping alive their original language.

The Maroons made use of the natural food sources available to them, creating the spicy dry rub and slowly cooking the meat over a smoking wood fire.

Today, locals and tourists alike visit the Boston Jerk Center, near Port Antonio Portland—the Garden Parish known for its lush greenery and deep turquoise waters.

To visit an authentic local Maroon settlement and discover the real origins of Jamaican Jerk, one must pay a visit to Moore Town located at the very top of the hills north of Port Antonio.

A trip to Jamaica just isn't complete without a review of the island's rich history.

Culinary Insight

1. A few drops of lemon juice added to simmering rice will keep the grains separated.

2. Never soak vegetables after slicing, they will lose much of their nutritional value.

3. To prevent cheese from sticking to a grater, spray the grater with cooking spray before grating.

4. A a little vinegar or lemon juice added to potatoes before draining will make them extra white when mashed.

5. When cooking greens, add a teaspoon of sugar to the water to help vegetables retain their fresh colors.

6. Cheeses should be served at room temperature - approximately 70 degrees.

7. Always use cold water for electric drip coffee makers. Use 1 - 2 tablespoons ground for each cup of water.

8. To keep appetizers hot, make sure you have enough oven space and warming plates to maintain their temperature.

9. To keep appetizers cold, set bowls on top of ice or rotate bowls of dips from the fridge every hour or as needed.

10. Always chill juices or sodas before adding them to beverage recipes.

12. To cool your punch, float an ice ring made from the punch rather than using ice cubes. It appears more decorative, prevent diluting and does not melt as quickly.

Best Food Spots To Visit 2024

- Best (New) Local Product: Smith's Rum Cream

- New Gastronomy Experience: Kamila's Kitchen (Skyline Drive)

- Jamaican Restaurant with Outstanding Gastronomy Experience: Miss Lily's at Skylark Negril Beach Resort

- Best Wine and Food Experience: Uncorked Sovereign North

- Best Watering Hole (Kingston): Raw Bar

- Best Watering Hole (Mobay): 27/27 Lounge

- Best Ethnic Restaurant: Mystic Thai

- Best Sunday Spot (Mobay): S Hotel

- Best Sunday Spot (Kingston and St Andrew): Jamaica Pegasus Hotel

- Best Place for Cocktails (Kingston): The Coppers

- Best Place for Cocktails (Mobay): Lester's Bar (Half Moon resort)

- Best Place for Vegetarian/Plant-based: Stush in the Bush

- Best Cafe: Café Blue

S Hotel: A Jamaican Oasis

S Hotel is more than just a place to stay; it's an engaging Jamaican experience. Nestled on the vibrant Hip Strip, this boutique all-inclusive offers an unparalleled level of comfort and hospitality. The attentive staff, led by the exceptional Manager, Andrès Cope, creates an atmosphere of warmth and familiarity.

From the moment you arrive, you find yourself enveloped in authentic Jamaican charm. The hotel's commitment to showcasing local culture is instantly evident from the delicious cuisine and lively entertainment to the thoughtfully curated library of Jamaican literature. I spent an entire day engrossed in "Roving with Lalah," finding myself captivated by the insights into everyday Jamaican life.

With its impeccable service and genuine spirit, S Hotel quickly becomes a cherished home away from home.

FISH

A Jamaican vacation would not be complete without experiencing the food culture. For seafood lovers, there are many fishing villages around the island where you will experience freshly caught fish, crab, lobster, octopus, shrimp. Watch these meals cooked on the spot, inhale the aromas, the different ways they are prepared—fried with escovitch sauce, steamed, jerk or roasted, served with breadfruit, yellow yam, green bananas, vegetables, bammy, water crackers, and/or festivals. While you wait, talk with the fisherman to learn about the different ways of fishing and other interesting aspects of Jamaican culture.

MARKET

You have to go to the markets and encounter the true Jamaican culture; the sounds of the patois (pronounced pa-twah) the colorful ways of describing things and people, music blasting as vendors announce the goods for sale, the mingling of colors, smell of exotic foods and fruits, aromas of food cooking. I could go on and on...

PAN CHICKEN

Jamaican Street Food is one of our regular go-to meals for quick, inexpensive, and delicious food. Especially Pan Chicken, the tantalizing smell of the smoke produced while cooking will make you salivate as you wait to be served!

ICE CREAM

A must have food in Jamaica is Devon House Ice Cream. Mainly because of its freshness of ingredients, number of flavors and uniqueness, Devon House is considered to be the number four ice cream brand in the world by Geographic Travelers list 2016. The National Geographic placed Devon House Ice Cream in their top 10 list for 2011. Moreover, "The Daily Meal" magazine lists it as one of the World's Best Ice Cream Parlor for 2017 at number 34.

RUMS

Rum is the national drink of Jamaica and used for various purposes such as medicine, cooking and entertaining. You must take a trip and taste the true Jamaican flavor that makes it considered by many as the number one rum in the world. Its alcoholic content is 63%, whereas it is exported at a much lower alcoholic content of 40%. Don't leave Jamaica without your rum.

CHINESE FOOD

Jamaican Chinese food is mouth-watering and a definite must. The large number of Chinese restaurants across the country is a testament to this cuisine's popularity amongst not only Jamaicans but also visitors to this beautiful island.

COFFEE

Jamaica Blue Mountain Coffee is rare and exceptional with a rich taste, full of body and a very smooth chocolate finish. The most expensive coffee in the world is grown in the Blue Mountain of Jamaica, which is the country's highest mountain range with altitudes between 5,000 and 7,000 feet. The climate is perfect for these beans which gives them their specialty bluish tint, and hence its

name, making it 100% authentic. Connoisseurs of these coffee beans say that its unique flavor is well worth the price. You are worth the indulgence of a bag of Jamaica Blue Mountain Coffee. The quality, flavor, and richness makes it hands down the best coffee in the world.

PATTY & COCO BREAD

In Jamaica, patty and coco bread go hand in hand. Locals as well as visitors to the island find Jamaican patties highly desirable. The flaky pastry filled ground beef that is seasoned with local herbs and spices is the most popular type, but you can also enjoy patties with other delicious fillings of your choice such as curry chicken, ackee & saltfish, vegetables, and even lobster (at some restaurant locations).

ITAL FOOD

Jamaican "Ital" food is the food of the Rastafarian. It is natural, organic, fresh, and straight from mother Earth. It is unmodified with no salt; usually a one pot meal made with freshly squeezed coconut milk, beans, peas, ginger, garlic, thyme, green onion, and an assortment of vegetables, and served with rice or yam, green bananas, sweet potatoes, Irish potatoes. This too is a must-have!

REFERENCES FOR JACQULINE FRANCIS

In the newspaper write-up of the
Third Annual Table Talk Food awards of June 2000

Jacqui Francis' contribution to the growing influences of Jamaican foods to the demanding palette of international visitors to Jamaica was noted in the following: Jacqui's love affair with catering began with her love to entertain and please her guests and create and ambience to enhance the enjoyment of food. She offers the concept of a mobile hotel service which brings the highest standard of Jamaican cuisine to the table. Ask President Chissanpo and he will again tell you "Thank you for your talent in preparing a so delicious a meal for us".

In a letter received from Managing Director,
Doreen Frankson of EdgeChem on March 22, 2006, she writes:

"We therefore thank you for the wonderful and appetizing meals provided that not just opened the palette, but satisfied the mind, Edgechem has always aimed for excellence and knowing that caterers, like yourself can meet this demand, is truly satisfying.

Letter from Prime Minister of Jamaica, P.J. Patterson of August 1997

Dear Mrs. Francis, the Emancipation/Independence Day celebrations held last weekend were both memorable and enjoyable. The reception hosted on Monday August 4TH, culminating the activities, and in honor of the President of Ghana, H.E flight Lieutenant. Jerry Rawlings and First Lady H.E Nana Konadu Agyeman-Rawlings was a pleasing occasion. The success of the evening was due in great part to the cooperation and assistance received from people like you. From the many compliments and positive responses which we have received, we are assured that your contribution did us proud in its display and quality. The products were savored by guests who could be heard giving praises and acclamation of the fine display. Please accept my sincere appreciation.

Award by Paget Defreitas, Editor-In-Chief, Jamaica observer limited

I have great pleasure to officially inform you that you have been selected among the nominees in the "Best Caterer" category for the Jamaica Observer's Third Annual Table Talk Food Awards to be held on Thursday, June 8th. As you are aware these awards are part of the Observer's efforts to recognize and celebrate excellence in Jamaica.

Reviews

Jessa Owens
Editor-in-Chief
ARPress

Chef Jacqui Francis has masterfully captured the vibrant flavors and rich cultural heritage of Jamaica in her book, "Nyam Thyme: A Modern Collection of Jamaican Recipes, Hacks, and Cultural Insights." This book is an absolute treasure for anyone who loves authentic Jamaican cuisine and is eager to bring a taste of the Caribbean into their kitchen.

Jacqui's dedication to her craft shines through in every recipe, each one meticulously crafted to ensure that home cooks can achieve the same delicious results that have graced the tables of state dinners and delighted international visitors. From the mouthwatering Jerk Shrimp & Lobster Jamdown to the hearty Jamaican Style Red Peas Soup, every dish is a testament to the rich culinary traditions of Jamaica.

The cultural insights interwoven with the recipes offer readers a deeper understanding of the island's heritage and the significance of its cuisine. These anecdotes and tips not only educate but also transport readers to the heart of Jamaica, making them feel connected to the culture with every bite they take.

Jacqui's personal touch, seen in her heartfelt dedication and acknowledgments, makes this book even more special. Her passion for Jamaican food, nurtured by her mother and grandmother and honed through years of professional experience, is palpable and inspiring.

"Nyam Thyme" is more than just a cookbook; it's a culinary journey that celebrates the essence of Jamaican culture. The New York Times should acknowledge this book for its exceptional contribution to preserving and promoting Jamaican culinary traditions. It is a must-have for anyone looking to explore the flavors of Jamaica, and it stands as a proud representation of the island's rich gastronomic heritage. Chef Jacqui Francis has truly outdone herself with this remarkable collection.

Dean Forbes

Global Publicist

Multilingual Communication Specialist/Translator

A Modern Collection of Jamaican Recipes, Hacks, and Cultural Insights" is a culinary masterpiece that brings the vibrant flavors and rich culture of Jamaica straight to your kitchen. Each recipe is a delightful journey through the island's diverse culinary landscape, offering a perfect blend of traditional and modern Jamaican dishes.

Jacqui's expertise and passion for Jamaican cuisine shine through in every recipe. From the savory Jerk Shrimp & Lobster Jamdown to the comforting Jamaican Style Red Peas Soup, each dish is crafted with meticulous detail and authenticity. The recipes are not only delicious but also accessible, allowing home cooks of all levels to recreate the magic of Jamaican cooking.

What sets this book apart are the cultural insights that accompany the recipes. Jacqui provides readers with a deeper understanding of Jamaican traditions and the stories behind the dishes. These anecdotes enrich the cooking experience, making it not just about food, but about connecting with the vibrant heritage of Jamaica.

Jacqui's personal touch is evident throughout the book, from her heartfelt dedication to her engaging writing style. Her love for food, nurtured by her mother and grandmother and refined through her professional journey, is palpable and inspiring.

Given the exceptional quality of this cookbook, it is clear that Chef Jacqui Francis deserves a wider audience. She should have her own cooking show or be featured on a well-known Food Network program. Her charisma, culinary skills, and deep knowledge of Jamaican cuisine would make her a fantastic addition to any culinary lineup, bringing the flavors of Jamaica to kitchens around the world.

"Nyam Thyme" is more than just a collection of recipes; it is a celebration of Jamaican culture and cuisine. Chef Jacqui Francis has created a must-have cookbook that will delight and inspire anyone who loves great food and cultural exploration. This book is a culinary gem that deserves recognition and a place in every kitchen.